Undiscovered

Debra Winger

B
WINGER

SIMON & SCHUSTER
New York London Toronto Sydney

Simon & Schuster
1230 Avenue of the Americas
New York, NY 10020

First Simon & Schuster hardcover edition June 2008

SIMON & SCHUSTER and colophon are registered trademarks of Simon & Schuster, Inc.

For information about special discounts for bulk purchases, please contact Simon & Schuster Special Sales at 1-800-456-6798 or business@simonandschuster.com

Designed by Jaime Putorti

Manufactured in the United States of America

10   9   8   7   6   5   4   3   2   1

Library of Congress Cataloging-in-Publication Data
Winger, Debra, date.
Undiscovered / Debra Winger.
p.   cm.
1. Winger, Debra, date. 2. Motion picture actors and actresses—
United States—Biography. I. Title.
PN2287.W496A3 2008
791.4302'8092—dc22   [B] 2007045252
ISBN-13: 978-1-4165-7267-1
ISBN-10:   1-4165-7267-8 (alk. paper)

Undiscovered

To David E. Outerbridge ~ who never relented

How to tie the ___ TRUE LOVER'S KNOT

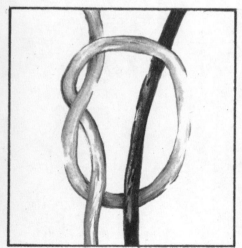

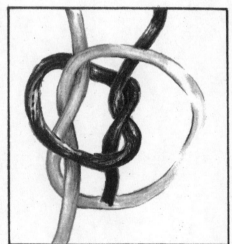

A.H., the simplicity is deceptive, as this bend is difficult to tie correctly. It requires less dexterity, so is often used in stubborn materials and is easy to do with wet hands. The tension keeps this beautiful knot in place. If tied correctly, it will never come undone.

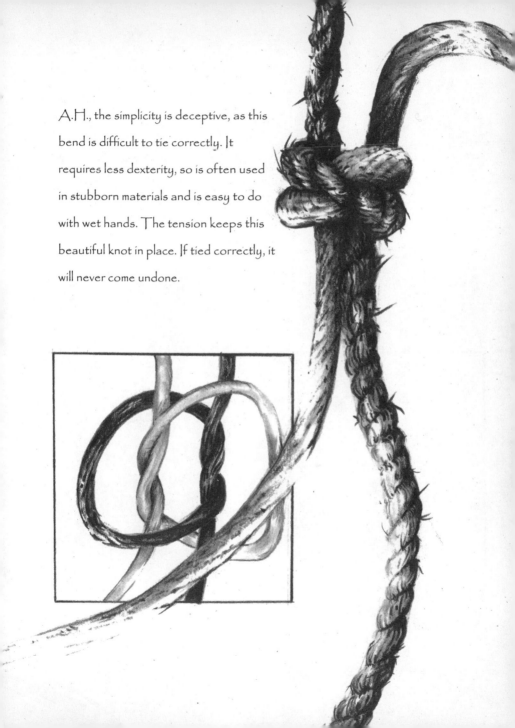

Arrangement of Spaces

Contents

Contents

Undiscovered

Preface

It is a beautiful spring day in May, and I am pruning my boxwoods. I planted them seven years ago with the intention of having a major topiary experience, but most years I find myself editing them to their most essential square. When pruning boxwoods, it is recommended that you not cut into the leaf. You must find the "Y" in the twig and cut it from there, otherwise you risk harming the shrub's growth. I find this small yet precise move, leading to a large overall effect, very familiar.

A dozen years ago the question of where I was going got louder than anything else in my head. My life had taken a certain trajectory into the world of films and stardom when I was quite young, and I hadn't stopped to question it. But in truth, it was like wanting a pony for your birthday and getting a big shiny merry-go-round instead.

Although I have participated in the odd film project here and there over the last twelve years, I had no real desire to hop back on that merry-go-round. I watched others as they grabbed for the golden ring and felt fine out in the country on my pony. It is a strange experience to be so *in* a certain world, and then *not*. I tried to imagine how to start anew.

I collected doors: odd ones from barns, farms, homes, and from my travels. I have dreamed of them in the forest, imagining myself walking through just the right one when I need a boost. I see them as thresholds to newness. Transformations *can* begin with a start.

Once, my friend and mentor James Bridges found me hiding under the covers, as I often did when I finished a job. I always felt that the roles I accepted must be inextricably linked to my life if I were to keep finding the passion to fuel each job. I had been to the desert making a film, and now everything in my life looked different. He quoted, "She took to her bed to lose her looks."

Charles Dickens, I think. It always made me smile. I could never quite decide if it was about the way the world looked at me or about the way I looked at the world.

I am always searching for the next door, the next role, the next change.

But right now I am pruning boxwoods, twelve to be exact, and I am wondering just how long it will take my mind to stop chattering and allow me to write. A fat red robin with the most laughably blue eggs in its nest is flying to the mud beneath the mailbox, hunting worms like letters from the earth. I want her to come and write this preface.

This morning in May, I am cutting boxwoods, pre-face and after-words on the threshold of my slender volume, with no in-structions, directives, or map—just a sort of pruning of a dozen years to their essential square.

Excerpt from
Shadowlands by William Nicholson

INT/EXT. BARN—OVERLOOKING

GOLDEN VALLEY—DUSK

In the shadowy barn, JOY and LEWIS collect themselves, wet but unharmed, and start to laugh. Then they become quiet again and look around. They watch the rain as it sweeps across the valley.

LEWIS

I don't want to be somewhere else anymore. I'm not waiting for anything new
to happen. Not looking round the next
corner, nor over the next hill.

I'm here, now, and that's enough.

JOY

That's your kind of happy, isn't it? It's not
going to last, Jack.

LEWIS

We don't need to think of that now. Let's
not spoil the time we have together.

JOY

It doesn't spoil it. It makes it real. Let me
say it, Jack. Before the rain stops, and we
go back.

LEWIS

What is there to say?

JOY

That I'm going to die.

LEWIS *finds this very hard.*

JOY

I want to be with you then, too, Jack. The only way I can do that is to talk to you about it now.

LEWIS

I shall manage. Don't you worry about me.

JOY

I think it can be better than that. Better than just managing. What I'm trying to say is that the pain then, is part of the happiness, now. That's the deal.

The Gateway Path

✳ Locustwood gate. Edible nasturtium. Upstate New York.

Birthday 1999

Forty-four years ago my mama waited in a car.

Maybe the window was down with the first warm night
of spring.

A dogwood might have been blossoming when my dad
stopped

to buy a pack of Camels

(she was so large with me not wanting to come).

Those were the years when the doctors were scared
thieves.

So frightened of a woman's labor pains that

they gave them the forgetting drug.

Maybe my ma, as she lay on that white hospital bed—

> needle in her arm

to make it happen—said things.

Maybe that doctor, sitting by her side, reading an article

> on abortions in China

from the *Time* magazine he found in the waiting room,

Heard all her secrets.

Maybe I did too.

Maybe it made me want to get out to give her some-

> thing to hold on to.

Maybe.

May baby.

A Moment

There is a moment in every day where some piercing clarity overwhelms the chatter of thoughts accompanying my body down the street and one, just one idea, wants so badly to become the seed of something written. Perhaps alone, or sometimes connected to a thought that was born in yesterday's bath, or one that sprang forth as a surprise ingredient while cooking. But it is written in magic disappearing ink. It slips away in the shadows. I occasionally get the haunting feeling that these ideas are all together somewhere, perhaps taking a mutant form of their own, from lack of nurturing. They need limits set, like a child does, to help them form. Now, released into a dark, mysterious place of the memory, they must find a truth that cannot live with the rest of the story. They are orphan chairs without a dinner table. My days will turn into a search for these lost connections—words to mobilize the world of thought. I am reminded of my childhood. There are not many actual memories, but one that surfaces has to do with language itself. Perhaps it is part of the plan to recover all the other missing words—somehow through moments in life, art as a verb, language can be a vehicle for vision and clarity.

I am a young girl, perhaps six years old, walking down the street. I am on my way to synagogue with my grandmother and grandfather. They are each holding one of my hands, and it is the Sabbath. We are walking through the big park, Cane Park, where I greet the policeman who can tip his hat without touching it. A sufficient enough mystery for a six-year-old. All the way to the old red-brick building that holds the services (about a three mile walk), my grandmother is sending secret coded messages by squeezing my hand at different intervals and for different lengths of time. I am entrusted to relay the exact same number and pattern of squeezes to my grandfather's hand. I am the conductor of a mysterious and important current. Perhaps this language was related to the sounds that I would soon hear in the service that represented a conversation with God; the thought occurred to me that the two were related, since I could understand neither.

It was not until years later that I learned (or perhaps just figured out) that these coded messages had no real meaning to my grandmother and grandfather. Isn't it strange that in some way they are still being interpreted years after both grandparents are gone?

In the place where this memory lives is perhaps the key to open all the other places that hold the stored words and stories that slip away. I am thinking this once again, walking down the street, writing in invisible ink. Will the thought of how to unlock the other words and live the memories for the second time (perhaps on paper this time) disappear into that other world of shadows and distant perfume? My mind seems to remember it but cannot actually smell the aroma. It is like the memory of a scent. Perhaps this memory can transport me to another state. Is that not as real? Is a coded message sent

through a young girl still a message, even though the transmit-
ters had no words attached?

Perhaps our initial contact with language actually has nothing to do with words. Much later in my life, I was told by a
woman who had a lot of experience with babies, never to pick
up your crying infant when you are angry and coo soft words to
reassure; better to leave the infant to cry for a little longer than
to pick up a being whose whole understanding of the world is
sensorial and give it this mixed message. What you are saying (I
love you, please don't cry, everything's all right) is the antithesis
of what is going on in your body (you are angry, defeated, and at
wit's end). These dueling realities can only lead to more confusion later on.

So now, when I sit to write, the first thing that is considered
is the unspoken, the place where all fear of the unknown and
exhilaration at the thought of the exploration exist together. My
desire, as I walk on down the street, chasing the elusive idea
written in invisible ink, is to find a piece of blank paper, light up
the shadowy places, translate the unspoken, and allow it all to
live together on the same page.

The nature of language is in its associations, its connection to events, or its ability to evoke. Sometimes the words on the page appear fleetingly, like they are floating in an old plastic 8 ball. I reach for the dictionary—a veritable orphanage of words, all ripe for adoption. Episode: "any event or series of events complete in itself but forming part of a larger one."

A part is played in a script. Lines are spoken—words written by an author but carried by an actor to their final destination. I try to remember being that conduit. There was the time in *Shadowlands* when I felt a terrible sadness at the end of each day—it came when I realized that I would never be saying those words just like that again.

Nothing Can Fill a Day

When I was sixteen, I wrote to a boy who had hurt me:

The warmth of your friendship
Has melted the snow
But now I stand alone in a
Great pool of icy water.

Nothing can fill a day.

Almost immediately nothingness comes in like light when the door to a dark room is opened. I count on things to dawn on me, the way shapes appear before the clear picture on an old television screen.

I lay in a hospital bed wondering if I would see again. My head had a distant aching, but I seemed to be hearing about it, rather than feeling it. My eyelids had that paralysis that comes right after a dream and before one is conscious. There is an anxiety, a need to "wake up," but the muscles will not obey. I had the feeling but not the anxiety. I did not want to awake just yet. I was aware that if I did, I would suffer. I could hear voices present but far away and was aware of some activity around my body. I could see myself.

I was in what others would call a coma, but for me, my eyes were turned inside out, and I was quite busy.

The fact that *Webster's New World Dictionary* devotes $3\frac{1}{2}$ inches to the word *troll,* and makes no mention of the creature that got me to this place, makes me wonder: Who decided that a "troll" was dome-shaped and wore size 23 Converse high-top sneakers? He's the one I should be suing.

But this was only a brief digression. Mostly when it became unbearable to hear my mother cry, I thought about what I would have to accept if I opened my eyes. At seventeen, I felt I had not really lived my own life—but rather a series of endeavors to please others, with few forays elsewhere.

I had a Christmas vacation job at an amusement park in Southern California to make some extra money. I was told at the onset how expensive my troll costume was and that I was responsible for its safety. So, in the California heat, fur suit removed, it figures that when I saw it slipping off the back of the small truck, I reached for it. At the moment I stood, the driver swerved.

As I lay on the asphalt with everyone fussing around me, it seemed, in slow motion, I saw what looked to be my body, rising up. I was also aware that I was still on the ground, unable to move. There were two or three of me now, each one a little more transparent. I wanted to be all together. I reached up with both my hands and somehow pulled me back. There. That was done.

Some Zen masters favor the technique of striking a student on the shoulder with a bamboo staff to have them focus on the "now." I don't think I would have felt the bamboo; it took an asphalt driveway. I needed that shock to the body. I needed to break completely with the ordinary life I was afraid of, but I did not know how to accomplish it. I didn't create the whack. It created itself. I understand it now as a fascination with what is unknown—a sort of dance on a high wire.

For years afterward, when people would say, "You had an accident," I would tell them it was not an accident.

Where I ended up, on the ninth floor of a circular hospital in the San Fernando Valley, made no difference to my state of mind. I was seeing myself for the first time, and that, too, was frightening. I had lived in a family that found work to pay for their lifestyles—neither one bringing much fulfillment. I was bound for this same road, ethics intact, no joy.

Time passes in a different way in this state. There were no days and nights as I knew them before or since. The organization of time seemed less linear and more spatial. I remember a realization that my condition was not altogether good, that something had happened that was causing my body to shut down. I didn't feel to let go into it, to relax. I felt the need to fight. And then there were my mother's tears. I don't imagine there will be many times in my life where such an extreme act of will, so clearly focused as it was, will present itself again. My first words, unfortunately, were to my mother, something unkind, as teenagers are wont to do, something like, "shut-up, please."

After a time, I don't know how long, I felt I could open my eyes. But I couldn't see anything. I was seventeen and blind.

For a while I thought I'd be the first blind actress. I had never acted before but harbored a secret longing. A dark cloud moved over me obliterating all of this hopefulness and desire.

My life became nightmarish now: pain, fear, and a darkness that went beyond any knowledge previously acquired in an unlit room. My eyes were cut off from the outside world, and one side of my body had to be sort of dragged along by the other side. I had no real idea how long this would go on. My intention became clear: I wanted to get beyond the sliding glass door, away from this place that was so familiar to me from routine doctor visits but had now become my prison.

A plan was concocted in my somewhat swollen head. I had surmised when it was evening by the shift change of nurses and the lack of visitors. I practiced. I would hoist myself out of the bed with the use of the overhead bar. I would count the steps to the door, walk out on the balcony, and jump. I plotted. It seemed like the rightest thing to do, and in my present state, the project became a challenge that excited me.

The time came that I felt the confidence I needed to pull it off. I waited, all day, and unbeknownst to those I loved, bade them farewell when they left. I got up, heart beating out of my chest, turning at all the counted steps I had planned, and reached for the door. Flesh. I was touching human flesh. Screams erupted, mine, theirs, others. I had successfully delivered myself right to the nursing station.

Why hadn't I heard the different sounds? Sensed the presence of so many people? What was at work that could thwart my noble efforts in such an abrupt and ridiculous way?

I never questioned it then, and I do not now. I collapsed, laughing hysterically, and was returned to my bed and considered a bit more unstable than before.

But, in fact, my stability was given to me that day. I was shot full of life. And as my sight eventually returned, I came to see it as a message from the universe. This is not your decision to make, darling.

The Approach

✳ Point of no return—the access for toreadors

to the Plaza de Toros. Seville, Spain.

Urban Cowboy

People give me things. When I go into a store now, there are samples, discounts, out-and-out gifts. It was not always so.

When I was cast in my first big role, I wanted only to be a documentation of the character, Sissy. No acting techniques needed—I would simply exist inside her reality, and they would film it.

I had spent most of the last couple of years at a small cabin that my boyfriend at that time owned in Ruidoso, New Mexico, a small mountain community not far from El Paso, Texas, and filled with drugstore cowboys and honky-tonks. I knew this girl.

I knew what she looked like and I knew what she was about.

I arrived at the Paramount lot the day I read about the recasting of the female lead in *Variety* (Sissy Spacek and John Travolta had a sort of falling out, I believe), with a story about how I had misplaced my portfolio. (What portfolio? A cigar-smoking agent had signed me while I was waitressing, but that only resulted in a blue movie.) They let me in.

I found the building where they were casting for *Urban Cowboy* and plopped myself down on the steps outside, trying to figure my next move. I didn't have an appointment like all the other actresses I would be competing against for the role. Two men walked toward the entrance, and I had to move aside. One of them, with rather tousled hair and a bemused look, asked me if I was there to interview for the part of Sissy. I squinted up at the kind face, and, in my best Texas, I replied, "Who wants to know?"

I went to Houston and worked the club scene. I was there every night, living what we would soon be filming. I was broke. I had paid my own way down, as there were still competitions and studio politics that I didn't have patience for, before I could have the part.

After the battles were fought and the director, James Bridges, with a loyalty I had not witnessed in my life, prevailed, we decided on a shopping trip. There had been long days of rehearsals and choreography sessions, and I had often sat on the stoop of my 3' by 5' cubicle in the "honey wagon," the trailer that houses all the dressing rooms, and stared out at Travolta's bus (on loan from Burt Reynolds) and marveled at the disparity of our situations. My entire salary was less than his per diem. But I loved where I was—I could smell something really good, and I was cooking it.

So John, Jim, and I went shopping. There was a huge western-wear store—we entered. Immediately the crush began. I slunk off to the outer corners, as Johnnie was being tossed lizard belts, ostrich boots, and 10X beaver hats by the rabid, half-crazed saleswomen.

As I made my rounds of the store, I could hear snippets of "Oh we'd love for you to have that, Mr. Travolta, our gift, it would be an honor" and "Please take that, it's great on you." I loved the openness and honesty of it all. He was sweet to all of them.

UNDISCOVERED

I had found the perfect belt buckle—the one I would end up wearing throughout the film—a little metal thing with a swirly "S" on the front.

I put it near the neat pile that had amassed on the counter. When we were all finished and things were being put into bags and boxes and some being worn out of the store, the saleswoman turned to me, off to the side, and through her tightest Texas lockjaw smile said, "Honey, that'll be $16.95."

I paid it, gladly.

Frogs

I was living in the Chateau Marmont when *Urban Cowboy* opened. I was too young and green to know about its reputation for being the last stop for so many actors and performers. It was in a location where I could walk to do the things I needed, which is not the norm in Los Angeles. It was ironic, then, that at the point I moved in, I could hardly go out. I had become recognizable in a somewhat rapid fashion, and I felt totally and suddenly self-conscious.

The character I had researched so deeply and the physical training I had taken on to be able to master a mechanical bull (as I saw it, a moving pommel horse) had been typified in many reviews, Pauline Kael's most notably, in *The New Yorker,* as a sort of sexy debut. It's hard not to feel that way after someone has said, "She wears her skin outside of her clothes." Sure I knew there was amazing suggestion in that scene, but to me the deeper truth was about what we do to impress the ones we love, and how misguided that need can get. I was crushed. How could they have missed my intention? To get inside this young girl's head: all the petty jealousies, the one-upping and the posturing—to bring the reality of life in a small Texas town in the 1970s, how could this have gone missing on them? How was I going to live with being considered the latest sexual flavor of the month, when what I really wanted was something small yet real. A pony. Not the goddamn merry-go-round.

My room was a converted closet. Bob De Niro was living in the room at the end of the hall, and, well, I was in his closet. I was living with my 120-pound Alsatian, named Pete. There was only room enough for one of us in the bed, and so the other one slept in the bathtub. Unfortunately for Pete, I got dibs on the bed most nights.

I had finished shooting *Urban Cowboy*, and the change it caused in my life was quite frightening to me, and so I spent most of my time in my room. I would sit and listen to the noises coming from the gardens outside my window. Some nights they were quite loud:

> The frogs stole my thoughts
> (they are every one of them a prince)

I started to write. All that I had to write on was a stack of lined index cards. The lengthy, somewhat mournful and altogether sentimental poem is still on those cards. I arranged them systematically on my wall, attached by pieces of Band-Aids that I found in the medicine chest.

> I see the parts
> the fragments taken to their hearts
> the split it caused in me
> this self-imposed exile
> Silence
> there is no one
> not even me
> who can wholly, this moment Be

UNDISCOVERED

I guess you could say that with very little preparation for something no one can really prepare for, I was thrown. I would venture out. On Sunset Boulevard was a large magazine stand—and if I could count five magazines in a row that did not have my picture or my name on it, I would continue on. Most days I turned back. *Urban Cowboy* had come out with all the attendant hoopla. I was a prisoner (of my own making) in a world I had not planned on, could not have conceived of. Reviews can be intimidating, even when positive. I was twenty-four.

Some nights I felt so lonely I would have a drink. I hated the taste of it, but it would help me to sleep. Petey didn't seem to care for this and licked my face to keep me awake. Some nights I just sat and wrote.

I felt the frogs to be my friends
   (within their singular croakful singing)
for certainly the telephone held no comfort with its
   ringing.

I didn't know at the time what it was that I found so difficult. The fame was one part, but I came to see that some of the trouble was the coming down from playing a character. I was not trained as others were, but there was nothing to do about it. Here I was, with opportunities and this burning desire to tell the stories. I loved the feeling of coming alive in a whole different set of circumstances, of seeing the world suddenly new, wild, full of possibilities. I just needed to recover each time.

"A bath cannot last forever," said I
"we heard the water draining and ceased our croak-
    ing," they replied.
"oh please, I'm frightened and so glad that you are
    here"
And with that, every prince, every one of them a
    frog, would disappear.

I emerged from that room with a plan that did not always include tactfulness. I cringe sometimes to think I had to be so tough to survive what was to be the next fifteen years of working in show business.

> I've seen them off, the frogs and my thoughts
> It is boring content right now that I fear

> I say to myself (as I am setting happiness up on
> the shelf)
> The frogs stole my thoughts; I haven't seen either
> one of them since.

I saved that poem somehow, and as sophomoric as it seems to me today, it holds the essence of what it meant to be so young, thrown into a world that was a result of the work I loved so much. I craved the work, not the celebrity, and I was willing to pay that price then. I eventually moved on from the closet to a whole room and went to work on *Cannery Row*. A strange trajectory here, because once again I was going to have to come face to face with the idea of objectification and "sex appeal," cast as a prostitute in the film, based on a compilation of Steinbeck characters from *Sweet Thursday* and *Cannery Row.* The absurd aspect of it, coming in as a replacement when Raquel Welch was not working out for the director and the studio, did not go missing on me. For those that do not recognize that name, the term "sex symbol" had to be created to make room for a certain need that seems always to be fulfilled in new and different ways. This can be confusing for a young girl with her heart set on telling her truth about a slice of life and not particularly concerned with what the pie looks like. The idea of fashioning myself to please men was a constant battle. Part of me loved that juicy feeling of being desired, but the attraction I felt to authenticity was far too fierce to leave me in that other place for long—and so began a very ambivalent relationship with acting in Hollywood.

One month into that shoot, I found it patently ridiculous to be driving to work every morning at 5 A.M. to stay in a beautiful trailer that was actually bigger than my hotel room, so Pete and I packed our bag and moved onto the MGM lot for the rest of the shoot. Perfect. I had 24/7 protection (the guard was a mere 100 feet from my door) and a commissary complete with a star-studded cast: Peter Falk was shooting a ladies' mud-wrestling movie; Richard Dreyfus and friends were rolling around in wheel chairs shooting *Whose Life Is It Anyway?* Steve Martin was shooting *Pennies from Heaven* in a strange hair-do; many, many, little people were dancing in *Under the Rainbow;* and George Cukor was with Jackie Bisset and Candice Bergen shooting *Rich and Famous.* All I had to do was sit on my front stairs. Every day was a parade.

The essence of those days stays with me and continues to resonate. I love the work and don't much care for the business.

Show Business

I was not too well acquainted with myself when I began working as an actress. I knew a lot about what I wasn't but had yet to learn what I could be. Consequently, I found myself shocked by much of what was expected of me. My success came relatively quickly, but I was terrified of doing banal work. I thought that if I did not stay alert, I would end up taking the easy route, and that would parlay into years of somnambulism: Rip Van Winger.

It's true that I sent a somewhat raunchy, often rude version of myself out there to deal with many of the indignities that film acting could provide. But just as in civilian life, often when one is met face to face with overt challenges, the warrior kicks in.

We had been working long nights and hard ones at that, on a film that, shall I say, was less than worth it. The budget was enough to feed *and* entertain a small nation, and yet it was not in evidence on the set—someone other than the people working all these hours was making it. Only the top percentile of working actors in films are paid handsomely, sometimes inordinately. I learned from one of my co-stars that in difficult times he would calculate what he was making by the minute, and that would get him through.

The director was not a people person. The script was no longer holding up under the acid test of production, and, as I said, the nights were long. We were about to take a much-needed break for the Christmas holidays and had one more shot to get. Inadvertently, a crew member backed into frame while working on some cables.

The director went ballistic. He screamed to everyone and no one, "Get that cocksucker out of my shot!"

A silence fell over the set, and the smell of anarchy mixed with the pine needles from the street-side decorations; that and the eggnog wafting up from the caterer's truck began to make me nauseous.

We broke early that night, a wise call on the part of the producers, for two weeks.

I guess we all thought that would be a sufficient amount of time to quell the adverse reactions to this man's assaults. We were wrong. Upon our return, one could feel a sort of anticipation in the air. Of course, an apology was not forthcoming, and it was unclear what would happen. The energy on the set was weird. I was called out for the first shot of the day, and by the time I arrived, someone had once again ignited the director's temper, and he was off, mouth running. When the shot was completely ready and everyone was waiting on me, I turned to the crew and asked, in a suitably loud voice, "So. How was all your cocksuckers' Christmas?"

The bark of laughter from my pals was worth what I would suffer later.

I found myself working with lovely people and difficult characters, with stunning directors and ones that stunned me. Slowly, not without grist, I saw the parts of the business that I could not abide. Acting was my learning ground: for characters, background, and skills. Research is sometimes my favorite part of the process. But the biggest lessons had come from love, and I wanted to experience the emotion at its purest. I was truly interested in how much reflection was generated by becoming a parent. I could not have known.

The first inkling I had about how all-encompassing motherhood would be came from the director Costa Gavras, who said when my first son was born, "They break your heart." Harsh, I thought. "Every day," he added.

I misunderstood him, of course, taking that breaking in a bad light. But the truth is, those words were profound, and the breaking is an integral part of what makes it so powerful. Having three children, born at ten-year intervals, had provided him with this information. He was telling me this over my swollen belly. In my ninth-and-a-half-month and sixty-third pound of pregnancy, he had paid me a visit to convince me to work with him on a film three months after I gave birth. Insane. Certifiable. I was so huge by this time that the only shooting I would qualify for was (1) a harpoon, (2) one of those telephoto lens shots of "stars gone bad," or (3) a "before" picture of something dire. He assured me that having something out in front of me would be helpful to me in the near future. How could he know?

Something about his sincerity and composure convinced me to bite.

And there I was, three months later, being handed my three-month-old son through the window of a car so that I could breast-feed him as the crew discreetly bowed their collective head in a strange tableau of silent prayer on the set. As I handed my baby back out the car window to continue the day's work, I felt the warmth of the soft flannel blanket as it left my hand.

My life had become full enough that I was able to see the metaphors up and running. Since those early days, I have found life on a small farm in the country to be closer to my nature than city or even suburban life. My favorite weeks at the farm were the ones where I turned everything over—no waste. I came to see that by cleaning up after myself and my family, I could read the story of my life. If the stories I was being asked to tell as an actress were not as compelling as the life I was living, I did not want to work. I had also grown weary of watching performances that seemingly had no life. I saw the trap of going from project to project and thinking that I could still bring the world into the film. I wanted a full life as well. In the hierarchy of the business, the further along I got, the more I found it difficult to get helpful feedback. I was so grateful to be able to meet wonderful artists and some intriguing businesspeople as well, but I did not find the joy in competition and the pain of rejection all that energizing.

Now of course, it seems as if my efforts flow more freely from world to world, and I am not so aware or dependent on the machine. I remember first hearing John Lennon singing about sitting there watching the wheels go round and round and making a wish for my life.

Barndoor Transformed

❄ Barn transformed with whiskey bottle transom and elusive cable.

Shokan, New York.

Irrevocably

Irrevocably imprisoned by a crush of immense responsibility, overwhelming and oppressive; and by a delayed upsurge of love that in the interim had grown so encompassing and so completely consuming that she knew that no matter how long she lived, no matter what she did or how, she would never ever be free again. She was a mother.

My Mother Was Great

My mother was great to me when I was pregnant, like pregnancy was a club and I was now a member. She pampered me, listened to my complaints with compassion and understanding, and offered up encouragement. The feeling that I had accomplished something without having had the baby consoled me when I would wake up in the middle of the night with hot swollen breasts and indigestion.

Birth stories were exchanged between her friends in my presence, although I wouldn't realize until later that they were vague, and certainly incomplete.

My mother wouldn't buy anything for the baby. In Judaism,

for the most part, it is considered bad luck to give a baby gift before the infant is delivered alive and healthy. Later, I found things had been bought and made but squirreled away until the appropriate time.

My son's arrival was late. Either he was comfortable in there, or something was "wrong," but after I had been carrying him for almost ten months, the doctor decided to induce. It took twenty hours of early labor with contractions that were unpredictable.

The first contraction that moved me from "labor" to "hard labor" brought me to my knees. Up until that moment there had been a party atmosphere in the room: my then husband and his friends, and some friends of mine, helping to pass the time.

When I lugged the sixty extra pounds back off the floor, I noticed my mother, who had joined in the party for the last six hours, packing up her things, and not without haste.

"Where are you going?" I asked her retreating figure, assuming that she was stepping out to the cafeteria to fortify herself for the next stage.

"Oh, I'm not staying for *this*. I know what you're in for."

Later I reasoned that perhaps she couldn't bear to see *her* baby in pain but that she was also telling me that now I had to stand on my own.

Ten years later, just before I became pregnant again, my mother passed away. She would not be there to hold the newest baby in her arms when I needed rest, a mother being one of the few people in the world who will hold your child sacred. Her support had been in her own style, but the very presence of your mother is sometimes the only support a daughter needs. This was not to be. I experienced a post-partum struggle that I hadn't faced in my younger new-mother days. I was blue, some days beyond consolation, and I wanted my mommy. Being a motherless mother feels unnatural. And I know that we begin to see our mothers in such a different light, first when we become a mother, and then when we lose them.

I long to watch my mother watch my sons. I now find myself with a very quiet version of my mom. One who doesn't criticize, overcook, or horn in. But it is also one that I cannot hug, cry on the shoulder of, or hand my baby to.

The Purple Color

Jim Bridges, in an effort to buoy my spirits, had set it up. I had become disillusioned with the business of movies—perhaps there was someone I could talk to about this burning desire to find out what I could not find out acting in film. Someone who might have a new idea that would not make me feel so out of the world.

I arrive wearing the wardrobe from the movie I am just finishing—a light lavender silk skirt and blouse, it being summer and California. There are no formal greetings, no classic introductions; just a growl from a bearded man in what seemed to me a tattered black suit—a gnomelike vision behind a dressing screen.

"Aghhh. Poor-ple: the color of Death."

All right, so it is not a great start, but as I have been well trained in the art of the quick change, I notice a dress manne-quin in the corner. We are meeting at the person's home in which he is staying while in the States; a seamstress I imagine. I quickly remove the dress from the form, remove my dress from my form and replace each with the other.

"A pleasure to meet you, Jerzy Grotowski, now tell me."

Jerzy's "Statement of Principles" for prospective students at his theater lab remains a more inspiring text than any script I have read. It reminds me that to find a way in an ever-deadening world is the ultimate challenge. The thought alone of striving to act without artifice was an explosion for me. A living master, with whom I could sync all that I yearned for with the extremes of success in the world. He was funny, warm, and ultimately one of the most serious people I have met in my life. I still can muster up the grin, the stroke of the beard. It's just that now, in my conversations with the man, I am wearing a purple dress, and he doesn't much mind.

Gardening

Gardening is much like directing. So much is in the casting—the passion that the actor has for the opportunity to tell the story. When I put a plant into my garden, if I place it incorrectly, I can water it, feed it, talk to it, coddle it, and not only will it not give forth, I may not be able to save it from dying. On the sunnier side (or shadier if that is what is needed), if a plant loves its place in the garden, it will not be stopped. You can feed it and help strengthen the blossom or intensify the color, but it will have no other imperative but to bloom.

The earth, as it spins now, is a pretty precarious place to live. I find that making changes of a smaller nature can often have a prismatic affect. Planning a garden is one thing, creating something from a dream. Watching it grow is another. A morning glory I planted one summer knotted itself over and over, and turned in on itself, and headed back down for its roots. I should have corrected it, but I was fascinated by the mistake. I was more interested in the metaphor.

We have a stand of poplar trees that people have been telling my husband and me will not last the winter. They have been saying that for fifteen winters now. I always sit in front of the window and watch the beautiful two-sided leaves applaud the first fall breezes. A curtain call, I think. But then, there they are once again, clapping in the spring. Underneath the trees that will not die is another story. No matter what I plant there, it will not thrive. When I have to go away, I return to a miasma of weedy vines and nondescript chokers. This year, after giving up for the last few seasons and letting the weeds have their way, I found some bright red, plump raspberries. What wanted to be a wild raspberry patch in a stand of poplar trees had come into its own.

Why does it take so long to uncover what seems so essential once it is revealed? I take turns in my life all the time. I feel an unshakable need to search, to dig deeper, to reveal, and to yield.

Throughout these years, I have tended gardens, and doing so is one of my deepest times for reflection. I have planted them upon births and deaths, although the latter takes me to the soil most naturally. In the melancholia of a colorful fall, when an ancient dread is brought in with the first hint of chill in the breeze, tulips, daffodils, crocus, any sort of bulb, can firm one's trust in the spring. No need for the panic that sends squirrels on suicide missions for a single acorn. Knowing the bulbs are there, sleeping under the snow, has helped me during those long days of dull white sun and single-digit winters. I guess moving to a place that actually experiences definitive seasons is a vote for metaphor. It is a hearty thumb up (hopefully green) to the knowledge that our brain cannot get us out of every mess that it gets us into. In fact, I often wonder if the brain's very nature is to keep us from acknowledging our other sources of strength, a ruler, tyrannical to the point of debating religion, acts of faith, and trust from the heart. All these issues can be found in the smallest of gardens.

Unmoored Confessional

❋ Abbey with dovecotes. Great Coxwell, United Kingdom.

Atchafalaya

I was in Louisiana on the Atchafalaya River. It was August 15th. My husband was shooting a film based on Faulkner's novella *Old Man*. I was driving through the bayou when I heard on the radio that it was the Feast of the Assumption; the day to commemorate Mary's being taken up to heaven, I believe. She was "assumed" into the Kingdom of Heaven.

Three months earlier, I had waited for my mother to leave her body. I held her as she breathed her last gurgling breaths, and then I kissed her and felt for her heart to stop. Soon it did.

And then I waited.

She seemed still there after an hour. Her body grew cold and her nails turned blue, but nothing was assumed.

The family became anxious to call and have her body taken away. N. beat on his paper cups with a laundry marker, as we had seen the drummers in Bali doing at a cremation ceremony some five years earlier; large, beautiful, handmade drums. N. informed my father that he was "beating Lama's soul to heaven."

But still, she stayed. Her face became set, and her body seemed to shrink before our eyes. My husband felt that perhaps because she was my mother, I might never feel her leave. This sounded right.

The thugs from the mortuary arrived in their Brylcreemed hair and their suit jackets that seemed made for smaller men. They put their rubber gloves on (my mother looked so innocent, so oblivious, and so unrequiring of rubber gloves). They wrapped her in a white sheet (good-bye face that I have known forever).

And still, I waited to feel some other part of her leave.

The soul must depart; what else *can* it do?

The tears of my father fell on the sheet as she was carried

out to a white panel van. We followed; I, hoping for her escape—thinking surely when she saw the mode of transport and her company, she would go.

They moved aside unrecognizable items strewn about, as if this were the last use for the van, perhaps a bowling ball in its black and red leather pouch, and put my mother and her body in the back.

And they drove away.

We slept, all three of us, on my mother's bed—sideways— too tired to think about it much.

Before we went to bed, I sat in the living room where she had labored and died just three hours before and stared at the bed I had rented from the hospital supply. It was stripped down to its rubber sheet and blue striped ticking. All of the metal underworkings were clearly visible. It had been such a mythic deathbed in the previous weeks, and now it was so crude and mechanical. I imagined it had always been both things; the largest most mystical and the smallest most ordinary thing; the linking of Quantum Physics and the Transmigration of Souls.

I could not feel my mother anywhere that night.

The next day, my brother, my father, and I went to the mortuary to work out the details of the funeral. The moment I entered the huge oak doors, I felt her. I knew she had not been alone a moment, given the orthodox treatment of being prayed over all night—that her *neshemah,* her soul, would not be left alone. Jews also believe that the soul does not depart until the time of interment—hence the need for a speedy burial.

I spoke to her silently, begging her to go—move on—that we would take care of it all just the way that she had wanted.

Before the funeral, I was taken in to identify her body before the coffin was sealed. The man lifted the lid of the plain redwood box, fitted only with wooden pegs, dust to dust; a thin, long casket expertly made.

There lay my mother, wrapped in a white cotton shroud and covered in a silly white veil that I am sure she would have disliked. I lifted it off her face and said hello.

Mama, what are you *doing* here?

The man from the mortuary excused himself, and I realized I was speaking out loud. I touched her. She was set now, firm and unlike any way that I had ever seen her in life. Jews do not embalm, so she looked quite real and completely dead.

But still . . . I waited.

We followed the rabbi out to the gravesite. My husband, brother, and four others carrying my mother away for the last time.

The rabbi shouted prayers as we paused three different times. I held my father and my son in each hand. How could this all have happened so fast? The blink of a third eye.

Today marks the Feast of the Assumption, the day Mary went up to heaven. I never did feel my mother leave, even when we, one by one, took the shovelfuls of earth to cover the box. I stared and waited and prayed. Already the Kaddish was being recited; the bid to move on, look forward, not down at my mother's grave and not up to heaven just yet.

I assume God has her.

January 23

I sit above an ice-encrusted earth—unable to move but for sliding back into ever deepening ruts in the yard. I have fought with myself for so long now. The voices inside my head were so noisy at times that I could not easily sleep or feed my family. It was hard to think of anything other than the constant talk of what will be, what will become of all of this.

I have played both parts—the leaver and the left; the betrayer and the betrayed. I have cast others in the role of the oppressor only to have them show up in the wrong costume or refuse to say their lines.

I desperately donned the apron and looked for the oven.

UNDISCOVERED

I stewed in the juices of disappointment and imprisonment.

I heard my mother and froze with the knowledge that she had not left yet—she was still in my house—trapped in my wedding dress, my maternity clothes, and my movie star gowns.

I have kept her with me, while mired, weeping in pools of melancholy—the echoing well of my grief.

Oh, Mary, mother of my mother's mother, what has kept you all from giving and living all at once? What has come to me, my inheritance, through years of unfulfilled dreams, from gods to husbands being blamed and disregarded? Why has this job been brought to me? I have worked all my life already. This legacy cannot be passed on—I will die with it, or it will die in my care. There are no more descendants, no girls dressing in their mother's heels and bringing out the make-believe dinner to unsuspecting dolls. There are no more unspoken angers, no more disintegrated violins or empty prayer books to sweep or hold up to the heavens as proof of life's betrayals.

The ice will melt and all will climb up. All must find their resting place away from my home—the sweet earth beneath this freeze will soften, and I will plant a new seed; everything growing up—toward the new big sky—food for the Feast of the Assumption.

Passover

It is the last day of Passover, and I am sitting in a Yiskor service on the Upper West Side. It is the service held for the dead, and I am trying so hard to invoke my mother's young face, but I cannot. I am still only able to remember the last few months as her body turned into an old woman's with the speed of time-lapse photography. I try to put myself in the home of my infancy, attempting to see her there. But all I can recall is the sadness I felt when we left for California in 1960.

I shake myself out of the drifting memories and pray for her return—to God and to my full memory.

I leave temple encouraged at least by my ability to feel compassion for my mother and for my grandmother (this part is just as important, I say). I walk down two blocks and look up to find myself stopped in front of a dress in the window of a small shop. It looks like how I imagine my mother looked when she was young. It is timeless and cheerful and full-cut.

I walk in, take the dress down, and present it to the saleswoman with my credit card; I do not care what size it is; I want it. She takes the card from me, and as she's ringing it up she casually says, "I thought I recognized that voice."

I hope for expediency. "I know your mother."

I say, "My mother? You must be mistaken. I'm not from around here."

"No," she answers, "I used to go to a dentist in Los Angeles; your mother ran the office. We would talk and talk. She is so proud of you and loves you so, and I feel the same way about my daughter, so we'd talk all the time."

"She passed away." The words just come out, I realize later, rather tactlessly. Tears shoot from her eyes. "I'm sorry, I didn't know. She was so young. I loved that woman."

I stumble out into the first bright sun of spring.

This, too, is what prayer can be—an opening to the world.

Mother's Day Gifts

I was amazed at how long my wimpy Mother's Day gifts had lasted.

Cleaning out my mother's house, I found a clay coil pot with an uneven blue glaze. I wondered why in the world it had not crumbled with time (once when my mother was so sick, I flew back to her childhood home and searched the attic for her violin—to remind her that she still could start something. It had been reduced to dust in a case); a construction-paper card heavy with glitter and lace—why hadn't it been shredded by now—all its poor workmanship glaring back at me (I sent my mother and a friend on a bus tour to see the New England leaves do their thing—she hadn't wanted to return, but the leaves eventually fell); a perfectly folded scarf, never worn (I remember my mother's knitting basket—a hobby adopted in hopes of becoming another kind of woman—I never remember a single knitted thing in our lives).

My Mother's Day gifts were so hasty, thoughtless, in a way. No content. A slipshod greeting for that day alone. I am sure I missed the chance to let my mother know how huge my love for her was. How much I needed, depended on, and appreciated her. I am sure I mismanaged my angry need to set her straight just one more time.

I finish cleaning and sit down on her bed—the culmination of three months of nursing, grieving, and now clearing out.

The moment is forever gone, and the flimsy gifts are what remain.

Abandoned Gates

☀ Cemetery in Sleepy Hollow, beyond the gates of a boarding school, Nemours, France.

Between Dreams

I am between dreams. That is how some days seem: just the time between. My mother is now present in so many of the dreams, but still unseen. Occasionally a voice, but mostly just the sense of her.

Yesterday I went to the garden with a blue ceramic bowl to see what could be gotten for a summer supper. The snap peas had joined at the top—two rows growing up the fences A. had painstakingly put up for me when I returned home from my mother's house out west. It was so important for me to put something in the ground so as not to have to look at a barren garden all summer and remember, in a sad way, the events of the spring. So snap peas were hastily planted, and here they were, grown clear over the fences and forming a little archway just over my head. I walked down the aisle and started gathering the fattest, juiciest ones in my bowl. I was instantly aware of pure joy.

It was exactly the same sudden happiness I felt when I was planting the little shriveled peas that constitute their seed. How thankful I am that enough child was gone to feel that planting had all the truths. The bowl of snap peas was the welcome but entirely unnecessary proof.

The City

I can count the buildings between my baby and myself when I am out in the city. I can sit and imagine every car and the lights changing from red to green. On a good day, I can imagine them all lining up green and the cars parting to let me through. Most of the time, though, they stay bunched in a group like some cartoon jam. The buildings increase in size and the wind howls in the opposing direction as I run home. I am not meant to be far away from him for this long.

Evgeny

I saw Evgeny Kissin play
on the night before his debut
at Carnegie Hall,
as if the eve of a great day
were more important.
The potential has an excitement
never realized exactly.
We sit together at the beginning
of so many years to come.
(yourfingersglideovermeonourfirstnighttogetherthey-
     donotweighathing)
He was so sure of all the notes,
His fingers did not touch the keys.

Penn Station

The woman I passed near the main board in Penn Station had such a familiar look on her face. I recognized it immediately: a roughly thrown together mix of anger, fear, and mounting horror with a little nausea slipped in at the end. I spoke. "Is anything the matter?"

She answered, almost at me, "My daughter. I can't find her." And proceeded to scream "A-sia!" while yanking her little five-year-old by the hand so hard she had to walk on tiptoes. "Aaaaaasia!" the tremble in her voice beginning to put a crack in her tough exterior.

The little girl echoed, in mock anger, "Asia!"

I said, "My son is just over there with our bags. I will send him over. Please describe your daughter to him, and he will go look for her as well. You stay in one place where your daughter might come back to look for you."

She was quite skeptical of the plan, but since it was the only one she had, shook her head and turned away for a quick yell, "Asia!"

I went to where N. and I had stacked our bags in order to check the ever-changing train board. He was sitting on his suitcase. I told him that this poor woman is frantic—that she shouldn't be moving—could he get her daughter's description and go look for her. I warned him not to go so far as to get lost himself.

Dutifully, he trotted off, and I watched as he listened to the information given, gave me a smile and a little wave, and took off.

I would say that within four minutes of him disappearing into the throng, a girl—much taller than I imagined—showed up and was promptly met with an agitated scowl from her mother. She seemed defensive, but in control. They looked over at me now, sitting on the bags, and the mother said, "Where's your son?" I answered for her not to worry, assured her that he would be back momentarily, and they all strode off.

So I waited. After five minutes or so, I began to have a vivid memory of being in Irian Jaya. N. was four then, and we were on our way to Bali. This was a stop-off for fueling in a country I had never quite placed on the globe. We had stepped into the building being used as a terminal. It was a one room, two-story creation, and it was absolutely jammed. A few planes from different origins had evidently landed within minutes of each other. There was loud music—drums mostly—emanating from one corner of the large, hangarlike room. Here, we found ten grass-skirted, bare-chested men and women with large rings made of bone in their noses, singing and beating on the drums. We walked some more, making our way through the tight crowd, and came to where some men were selling spears—primitive and absolutely huge—from a barrel. I picked one out to show N. and turned around, but he was not there.

UNDISCOVERED

In the quarter-hour that we were separated, I came as close as I ever want to understanding completely what life would be like if someone stole my child. Several planes had started their engines and were preparing to take off, taxiing down a short runway—visions of slave trading and illegal adoptions swarmed into my head.

I had to stop those planes.

When we were reunited through the kindness of a couple who had stayed with him until we found each other, we both cried in each other's arms and proceeded to have an exquisite trip to Bali.

Back in Penn Station, where mobs of people are crowding the main floor area, I flash on the possibility that I have traded my son for this woman's daughter, to some invisible, unknown agent of past scores. I begin to whistle loudly and then, finally, to scream—much like the woman I had come across a mere twenty minutes ago. I have shed my public traveling demeanor completely (a quiet, hidden face in the crowd) for this hollering, frantic mother in distress. I am just starting to formulate an elaborate plan that includes most of the NYPD when N. walks up behind me and says "Mombo?" I turn, and just as *he* used to do when he was an infant, I dissolve in tears of relief, at the sight of his questioning face.

"I thought I heard you calling my name, but I was looking for Asia."

The Plough

I woke up five times, six times. I dreamt that my dog of fifteen years, Petey, was in the hospital and I had to get to him, but my efforts were being thwarted by bad directions, getting lost, having to backtrack. I did not know where I was, lost my phone, and grew desperate. Every time I woke, I told myself, Debra, go back to sleep and start where you left off, with all this new information, you'll get there. Every time I fell back asleep, something new and worse would send me backward in time, and instead of getting closer to the hospital, I was getting farther away. The more I would rush, the longer it was taking.

In the freedom of the dark, the mind may move in many

directions. I feel split and maybe split again—each one lost from the other. Slowly, steadfastly, through the night, I collect myselves.

I had a daughter named Laura for a short time. She was the granddaughter of a man I knew, and as she got a little older, she began to refer to me as her godmother. I cherished not only the title but the opportunity. And her. She was an amazing young girl with an awful disease. She lived life as fully as one could, and when she passed away, that day, she became older than me. Someone I now turn to in the darkness, in the confusion of a dream-filled night, when I cannot make sense of time. It turns around and comes back on me. I am the smallest, and in my dreams again I am searching through time, through hospitals, through all that I have known, for those I love. Have loved. To once again care for a young girl, bury my face deep in the fur of a dog's neck, be able to help in some way that I could not figure out when they were here.

In my dreams, I often do not reach my destination. I awake in the morning, mournful. The light of the day slowly puts time in some order that my nighttime family will not cooperate with.

Seasons appear but do not matter to them. I return to the countryside. House of dreams, house for real.

The fall is falling. The last of the hay has been baled, furniture put away, bulbs hastily thrown into the ground, the road to the house smoothed and graded for the unforgiving blade of the plough.

Limbo

Recently, the time I have experienced as "limbo" is the time spent driving a car with a sleeping child in the back. Whether one has used the car as a lullaby tool, or simply found themselves going from point A to point B (however pointless it now appears) and glanced in the mirror at the back seat only to discover a formerly cranky, overheated bundle sawing twigs peacefully and quietly, the moment becomes a sort of limbo. You are driving and yet there is nowhere to go. You are reluctant to move forward, and you know why. Suddenly, Time opens up and swallows you whole.

These times during the old days, the single days, the loose

foot days, before you gave every moment up to a cell phone, could deliver you to an epiphany, a state of clarity, or at the least, drug rehab. But these days, anger and exhaustion are most likely the rule. However, if you manage to get through all that and still be driving, something is possible.

I had a limbo moment the other day. Driving around New York City, I found myself wondering how I got there. Yes, the Deegan Expressway was the first landmine to elude, and several ranting and self-help epithets after that; but B. continued to do his impression of an angel, and I lifted up. Up, out of my car stuck in midtown traffic, up, out of New York City, up up up.

Ten years before, when we were in Florida, they let us see the launching of one of the early space shuttles. I was mildly interested, but space only really interests me when I can reside there. The guys felt quite differently. We watched as the countdown activities proceeded and as the huge fires began to grow and the smoke billowed. I figured the reason I wasn't that excited was a gender thing. The shuttle started to lift off and was quite impressive as far as big things getting off the ground are; it gathered speed and was really shooting up now. People were applauding and cheering. I kept watching until it was hardly visible, and then it happened. After all the up up up, it turned. Just like that, it turned and shot out of sight; so clearly off to a place I did not know.

My breath went with it.

How could it be that there would be no words to express what I felt?

The chance, the opportunity.

The foot on the wire suspended in space.

There is a sound in the car. A sound so heartbreaking I try to keep holding my breath so as to hear every ounce of its tone. The child speaks his sweet sleepy greeting as he comes back to this world.

Roof Hatch

❉ Stairway to roof terrace. Marrakech, Morocco.

Sheltering Sky

At this point, apart from a gnawing desire to be close to Belqassim all the time, it would have been hard for her to know what she did feel. It was so long since she had canalized her thoughts by speaking aloud, and she had grown accustomed to acting without the consciousness of being in the act. She did only the things she found herself already doing.

—PAUL BOWLES, *THE SHELTERING SKY*

Occasionally, there is a feeling that the whole of your life has brought you to a certain moment. As if it were a series of vehicles that you transferred between, and all at once, you were dropped off at a certain place, and the car sped away and left you staring into the void. Such was the sensation, arriving in Africa to film *The Sheltering Sky*. Equipped with years of acting experiences and a three-year-old, I didn't look exactly ready for a sojourn in the desert. But looks can be deceiving. I was so ready that I surprised myself with a fearlessness that scared me.

I had felt for years that I was being pursued, and I kept moving faster to outrun whatever it was. I didn't want to know. Motherhood had caught up and overtaken me, but now, it was something else. Standing at the edge of the Sahara, all my un-written poems caught up with me. There was nowhere to flee. I at once felt the vastness of the universe and each grain of sand.

Bernardo Bertolucci hated it there. He stood next to me one day, pointing to the expanse, and explained that he did not even like going to parties unless they were thrown *for* him. I, on the other hand, had had my fill of false celebrity and the prying in-terest of the press. I arrived at that sandy precipice and loved it.

It is hard for me to say how much a character's virtual life experiences affect my real ones or vice versa. I was busy working with a script in hand, but it was not the film, rather life itself, on the edge of and into the heart of the desert that was the biggest awakening I had had since I was seventeen:

> I am here in this room because everything I have done in my life has led me here. Every sign read, every path chosen. That which presented itself and was not fought back or negated by my fear has brought me to this small, quiet room atop a village in Africa. Sounds of distant music and the constant barking of a dog somewhere below. The music ceases. Some night birds very faintly call. No trace of daytime activities. The sound of the dried mud every so often falling to the floor. What is that movement? The breeze causes it to slowly disappear. This is really the essential element. Air. Which changes all things. The first stirrings of dawn. Women and water.

UNDISCOVERED

My life was changing inside of the film. I had felt this before, but always, in the decompression after a film, it dissipated. Now, in this moment, I am aware that the experiences are actually being taken in differently, as if by someone else. The change has come.

Out in the desert with no persona to speak of, I
find unimaginable joys. I am neither held up to
any prior expectation nor must I feel compelled to
begin a whole new one. This liberation is almost
unbounded. At once I can let go of the handles to
all of my baggage; to the thoughts, memories, and
ideas that weigh inside of them. Inside this world
of my chech and robes, inside this mud room, I
can be without.

As with all transformations, there are certain qualities that return to a familiar, habitual way, but the gentle shifting is seismic and affects the whole of ones' life.

It occurs to me now that so much of acting is undoing. At least for me it is. I seek to go to the edge of what I can know about a situation or a life and then undo the rest of me. Set it free. When I was first starting out and heard all the stories of actresses being "discovered," I decided I loved the word. But not for what it had come to mean to others. I loved it in a real life sense. I have a photograph of myself at about twenty-three, foot up in the air, arms open to the universe, proudly wearing a tight T-shirt that reads "UNDISCOVERED." I saw my life and my pursuits as an uncovering of who I could not know I was until then. My young life had not supported such daring, and the examples were not in evidence. If I was to end up in places I could not yet imagine, I needed to undo some of my thinking.

And, although since then, I have learned many ways to this end, I knew that this trip to the desert, this film, at this time in my life, could be my undoing.

Ultimately, these experiences that become infinite in nature also belong to the finite world. They live as a memory of the possibility of transformation; transformation through blunt, quizzical, and an emotionally honest look at the life around us, at ourselves—our lot. The possibility exists for all of us, at any age, to imbue our days with a breath fully taken, the thought fully formed, and the emotion wholeheartedly felt. How often do we? We are full of undisclosed fear, unexpressed resentment, and a feeling that there will be a time in the future when we will get to it.

I knew, at the end of *Sheltering Sky,* that a combination of environment and work that I love would always be my ticket into a new experience of life. It has created a yearning that can also wreak havoc on a creative mind. Living with this double-edged gift is a precarious balance. But, that's the deal.

Thatched Passageway

※ Hotel hallway with thatched roof. Thebes, Egypt.

Simplicity

There is a simplicity to February. There can be no snow, and the days can be bright. The orchard can be so clean, no leaves to confuse the eye. No weeds among the berry bushes. So little to mind—the wind blows sharply down the short rows, picking up only the stray twig broken off from the last ice storm.

I am grateful for February and its stark, low-maintenance appeal. I do not miss the loud green sprouts sleeping under the surface—they scream of need and ideas and clutter.

I can go out today with questions—only questions—and

live with no reply. Let them sit out there in the empty cold and blow up against a rock. I don't care.

I don't want to be forced to gather all the evidence that nature can leave lying around in the spring, all the not-so-subtle hints of God. All the color proofs and loud hymns.

I want this question mark that is February.

Asteroids

My twelve-year-old son is explaining to me his idea of how to build a deflecting device for an asteroid bound for earth. It is evidently hurtling toward us as we are speaking. I am collapsed in an unlikely chair in the corner of the kitchen, a chair no one sits in, a chair that affords me a perfect view of my two-year-old son, who is quietly and rhythmically transferring each pebble of the dog's food from the dry bowl it has been in to the bowl of water it will now dissolve in. I say, do, nothing. I am really trying to follow the technical specifications that are being so vividly described. The dog has been doused with tomato juice and still smells like a skunk. The fish crackers have been vacuumed from the sofa, and the mice that have been leasing the bag of birdseed with an option to buy have been given an eviction notice, post mortem. I have made this choice to raise my children in the country for now, but sometimes the humor escapes me. And although I know this will all, in one heaving sigh, become part of the ether, the very air that someone reading this will breathe.

I cannot move.

Gravity has stolen whatever reserve of strength I possessed.

Summer of 2000—the Dream

We drive at twilight over winding country roads past the farmer's fulfillment—a warm day—bundles of freshly mown hay wrapped in its modern white plastic sheaths, looking like giant balls of mozzarella cheese waiting to be transported to some musty old barn where they will sit until the dead of winter.

Plastic bales depress me, I think, looking out the window. If they appeared in my dreams, what would I think they meant?

"I would like to find some work I really love." There it sits, having rolled off my lips and just as out of place as white rolls in the middle of a hay field at twilight. A sign of the times.

"Daddy," our three-year-old son says, "now you make a wish too."

His answer comes immeasurably faster than mine would have.

"My wish is for Mombo, when she comes down to Mississippi to be in the film, to find some work she really loves."

And what is your wish, son? On this magical evening, driving with both your mom and dad, safe in the knowledge of their love and admiration, soundly cradled in the adoration of their affections, carried on the soft cloud of their devotion and support. What is your dream?

The answer comes.

A train is involved, and it is a wish so simple to fulfill that my mind already plans the ins and outs of it all.

Broken Crockery and Howling Dogs

Consider this: There is more to wed than the lock.

One August, I abandoned my riding mower before the front field was finished. It's not that I didn't want to mow the entire field; it's just that it got too noisy. After I walked away and looked back, I felt kind of bad. I thought my husband might see the psycho pattern in the rye, the tufts left high, the figure eights, and wonder if I was someone that he would be tending to soon.

I learned a while ago that all you really need to know about a person's state of being can be revealed by how they mow. I have been caught working out some fundamental problems on a mower. I have been guilty of sending messages in the grass, condoning my uneven behavior with uneven rows, and calming my nerves by smoothing it all over in the end, like sweeping the dirt under a grass carpet. In the countrysides, world wide, people mow, thrash, burn, and otherwise attempt to tame nature. They do it joyfully, dutifully, angrily, in haste, and as art. I did it all those ways. But this time I wasn't really finished.

I was trying, that hot afternoon, to elicit mercy. To woo it, to will it, to feel the warm relaxed wash of its descent. I couldn't seem to do it wholeheartedly with the loud engine of the mower muffling my incantations. I thought if I left the prayer in the grass, maybe it would be spotted from above. But I abandoned my pursuit in some existential anguish, embarrassed to be so rudderless, without a plan, after so many years of marriage.

Once you have started with mowing as a form of communication, it is hard to move on from there. You begin to think of similar means to settle disagreements. I have always hated the thought of broken crockery. The howling dogs almost always closely follow the sound, and the cacophony ends up deafening any worthwhile discussion.

In suburbia one can start making love every time a leaf blower is fired up. If you know suburbia, this is a real fine suggestion.

But here I am, with this rural mess of a field. The gestures are rampant, and the results are fitful alien landing pads. I am sure he will go out there in the night and make the rows go right. Show me how it is all going to be working out well, very soon. Go on, I say in my way, I dare you to love me. Fast, before the grass grows.

After sixteen years of a promise, it is easy to forget what the vital signs are. The daily life tends to carry you in its flow, and it takes diligence to make it stick. The degree of difficulty can be squared again and again by the bringing together of children, loyalties that preceded your union, mistakes made, and any form of housework. I know staying together is not the difficult part; hell, the world is strewn with compromised relationships, unfulfilled people, and complaints. Any successful marriage takes a devotion to irony that borders on Zen. I am hoping, at this stage, that faith leads to mercy; and I don't mean either of those words in a religious sense. I am just thinking that since I have been faithful and my devotion has been heartfelt (if not always cheerful), I can find mercy on a riding mower if that's where I need it.

So it's back out to the field. Today's irony being that a woman with two sons and one stepson should not have to mow. But I want to say something I cannot find the words to express—not from shame or fear, but more a yearning for a whole new language to translate the next section. Authenticity is not a goal for the faint-hearted. I have started on this journey, and I want to continue with grace.

The mower won't start. The fog is so thick at 6:30 A.M. that I can almost hold my hand out and watch part of me disappear.

I wander to the barn, praying for the sound of a distant leaf blower to send me back to my conjugal bed. I pick up the rusted scythe that my husband found with some other antiquated tools I have come to love for their silence. The back and forth motion and the absence of a revving engine turns out to be just what my body needed—the calibrated swinging says, be even Debra, be calm, and for God's sake be quiet.

Ted Kooser +

Today, as I got to the bottom step of my basement stairs, having painted the entire flight a dusky Moroccan red, I realized that my husband was gone, the storm door was locked, and I was surrounded by twenty-eight boxes that had arrived after my father's recent passing, containing a record of most of my childhood and all of my professional life. Whenever I am presented with a metaphor this stacked, so to speak, I ask myself what would Ted Kooser do?

I have reported to Ted through the years about daily tasks and reflections that I think others would find mundane. His life inspires me to see beyond the duty and into the joy. Mowing the lawn, taking care of an entire family with the flu, or having a perfect recipe dissolve into mush could have been reason enough to go AWOL, but as long as there was a letter to Ted in it, I was saved. When I was researching colloquialisms, he sent me four books on the subject with titles such as *A Hog on Ice* and *Heavens to Betsy.* His appreciation of a life well lived *and* articulated relaxes me when I am verging on a full-blown existential anxiety attack about my accomplishments.

Over the years, Ted has discovered the United States Postal Service will pretty much accept any flat object as long as the stamp covers its weight. Bingo cards, instructions for constructing an "Indian raft," paint-by-numbers (acquired by Ted, with an expert's eye, at garage sales across Nebraska and into Iowa), all transformed with a simple vertical line, address on the right side and a short explanation, poetically rendered, of the history of the object, on the left.

Inside conventional envelopes, I have told things to Ted that could only be written to a person who lives in metaphor.

Once when I was trying to describe a planned walk by Philippe Petit across the Grand Canyon on a high-wire, Ted wrote to me: "Nobody can describe the Grand Canyon, but somebody can describe how a little boy looks who has just found a nickel on the floor of the Grand Canyon. And leave it to the editors to check the spelling and grammar and clarity. These are the people who follow the parade and clean up after the elephants."

Recently I was re-reading some older work of Ted's. There was a hint of nostalgia in my action. I was feeling conflicted about this new Ted Kooser + (as I refer to him now—the plus standing for Poet Laureate of the United States). I haven't received a letter in many months. I know I am to share him with the world now, but oh this year seems hard. I know he'd understand; as he observes, it's the moment when the

> Kite bounced along on its tail
> Then shuddered and lifted itself
> And shook off its own surprise.
> —"For Jeff," *Weather Central*

UNDISCOVERED

And so, this year, I may not get any little pieces of cardboard that were "used to separate the individual pillows of shredded wheat in the box—how lucky we are to live in a world where there are millions of small marvels—words printed inside matchbooks, little slips of paper put into our pockets by clothing inspectors with numbers for names," but how lucky I am to write this little missive for my favorite National Treasure.

Ted once told of coming home from a radiation treatment, and as he neared his home, lined up on the fence was a sight he had never witnessed before: vultures, hunkered down, wing to wing, the length of his yard. He stopped the car, got out, and addressed them.

"Not this time, fellas."

I am so glad he told those eager misanthropes off.

People and Place

At the veterinarian's, I watched as he pulled porcupine quills out of a dog's snout. I always like going to the country vets for their weird sense of humor. I guess if you can put your whole arm up a cow's rectum, you have got to be able to laugh. If you ask a country vet, as I did regarding my Alsatian, Pete, "Can he live with just one kidney?" he will undoubtedly tell you, "Yes. Just as long as he doesn't get shot in the other one."

As I leave this vet's office, he slyly says to me, away from the dog owner, "That porcupine breeding I took up last year is really paying off."

I leave, happy to be living where I am living. In the summer, the influx of people in, say, convertibles and high heels, changes the feeling of the towns, though the Catskills are still lush and comfortable. I have been here about seventeen years—first full time and now back and forth. It is hard to know a place unless you are in it through all the seasons. Some people, I know, do not think it necessary to feel this sort of connection with place. I think to know a place truly is one of the deepest lessons of existence. Sometimes, meeting older people out here, I am overwhelmed by a lifetime of events I may never hear about that are at play in their eyes.

As I am driving home from the veterinarian's, I stop at the sight of a crudely drawn BARN SALE TODAY sign. I pull off to a somewhat dilapidated barn with a lot of junk in it. As I am sifting through some things on a table, I lift up a knife. There, on its bone handle, is a small swastika. I immediately replace it and look over at the man whose barn this is. He is seventy something. I ask him where he got the knife. There is nothing alarmed about his response. He says, "It's only a replica. Why? Does it bother you?" The latter is said without antagonism. I am not interested in pursuing the conversation.

Once, back in 1985 when I was on a world tour with Jack Nicholson for *Terms of Endearment* (how the two of us swung that, looking back on it now, I'll never know), we were on a plane bound for Germany. I had never been there and was relentlessly joking with Jack about how I, as a Jew, would be treated. I told him that if they put us in separate buses at the airport, he should call my parents and let them know. He finally told me to stop, that these paranoid fantasies had little to do with modern Germany and that I should relax and enjoy the trip—perhaps join him on his search for the perfect brothel . . .

When we arrive at the hotel, an amiable man who looks to be in his sixties greets us. He shakes my hand, and it freezes in his. I quietly pull my arm away and avert my eyes. Where had he been forty years earlier?

When Jack gets up to his room, I receive a phone call. "Bucky? [his nickname for me] Is your radiator making a hissing sound?"

How can a place be completely different, when the memory of events still lives in a handshake, behind the eyes of a stranger?

I leave the barn and say goodbye to the farmer running the sale. It is not his fault what he lived through, but I do not want to think much more about what that knife "replicates."

The mist of the morning is starting to dissipate as the bright shafts of sun push through the tall firs. The road winds, and the light strobes, and there is the sense of no time. All the stories disappear into fog. I stop the car, and the deer meander toward me. No one runs. Nothing to fear.

I drive on past G's house. He is a sheep farmer here and recently lost his wife of forty-seven years. I have been dropping off soup and the occasional dinner for him, so that he can work all day and have his food ready when he comes in, the way it used to be. But as I stop to talk to him, he looks adrift to me, the ship of his partner having sailed. He tells me he is not sure why he is doing it anymore. And then he asks me if I am familiar with the Bible. He looks back up to his barn: "We are all vapor."

I drive on through the hills, wondering how to keep interested in it all. To know a place, as well as people, but to forgive all the stories the way we do weather. To just keep on through the fog.

When I was quite young, but old enough to be living on my own, I fell hard in love with an actor. We met on Yom Kippur, at a screen test for a movie (neither one of us got) to be directed by Stanley Donen. At the end of the scene I was reading with this complete stranger, Mr. Donen asked us to kiss. Well, that kiss was electrifying. He finally yelled "cut" for the third time and told us to get a room. As Stanley ushered us out, he slyly said, "What's a nice Jewish girl like you doing in a place like this on Yom Kippur?"

We spent the next two months never leaving each other's side. He had a little place in the mountains above the Pacific Ocean. I moved in, sure that this was to be the man I married. It was a strange dwelling, built from old sets of Shangri-La in the movie *Lost Horizon*. He rented it from set designer Tony Duquette for a price even I, broke at the time, could afford half of. It was originally a trailer, extended by the addition of a large glass room. Watching the moonrise from there is one of my most vivid memories. Here is another.

One day his best friends were visiting. A couple that he had known for some years. The guy was a striking blond actor, muscular and very cheerful. The woman was a model for the Olga underwear ads. Perfect, in so many ways that I was not! The day they were visiting, the guys had some project they were to be working on. I was out in the garden holding the hose when I suddenly dropped it and walked inside. I never knew what compelled me to make that move, but when I entered the house, framed perfectly in the window to the connecting trailer was my new love, locked in a passionate kiss with his best friend's girlfriend. Stunning.

I found myself wondering for years afterward why betrayal seems so predictable to me. Why waiting for the other shoe to drop was just a matter of course, never realizing that it was no way to live. I always seemed to understand characters that had their dukes up before anyone was ever punching. How many times had I fled to avoid it?

I often think that the feeling of betrayal I have about the current political situation so easily dispirits me because of my past. Why does the philistine nature of America's power brokers so easily work as a soporific? Is it the same weird expectation of betrayal at work? What is the sound of one shoe dropping?

Betrayal can live inside of you like a poison that feeds on disappointment. It is completely useless for life in the now. It must be mined and wept about and turned into a story with a beginning and an end.

I am driving through the lifting fog. I am so grateful for my life. I will try to awaken all the parts that can be useful out in the world. I am happy when the past stays put, but for a tale well told. I will drive up the long dirt path to my home, pick up the garden hose, and water my garden today.

Tall Girl

The shop is called "Tall Girl." I stand there wondering if I walked in and started sifting through the racks, how long it would take the salesgirl to gently break it to me that I would, in fact, never find a thing there. It is two weeks before my son's thirteenth birthday, and he has worked for a couple of years toward his bar mitzvah. I decide the occasion calls for a new dress, something I have not given myself since my mother died. Shopping just wasn't the same without her to tell me exactly what she thought of the purchase.

My grandmother wasn't much of a shopper. She had one blue dress that she wore to weddings and a black one for funerals. Whenever I told my grandmother who I was dating, she would ask if she should take out her blue dress.

UNDISCOVERED

I have threatened my son on several occasions that if he does not do his work and study hard and reflect mightily on the significance of this day, I will show up in a tight red suit with a mini skirt. Satin.

My strategy may be working; he is astounding me at every turn with his devotion, earnestness, and sense of purpose. The fact that I am spending the better part of my days figuring out how to get port-o-potties into my backyard so that the celebration does not culminate in a backed up (already temperamental) sewer system does not go missing on me. I am happy for my son and his passion for whatever he is doing. I want to stand up and say Yes, I am his mother, and I was there, watching, while he did all of this himself. I want to be able to do all of this without turning into an emotional wreck.

I leave the mall an hour later. On the way to an appointment, I realize that I have bought a blue dress. All that I have put off will have to be done in the next week. It will be nice if the guests' feet do not stick to the newly painted floor. The more I try not to think of my mother in this context (is it a coincidence that the party falls on Mother's Day?), the more ridiculous this seems. I decide that I must have something for every mother who will be here on this special day. As I am selecting fifty-four of the nicest lotions and picture frames I can find, it occurs to me that I really only wanted to buy one gift. But those days are over. Evidently, so are the ones where you can just park a port-o-potty anywhere you want. The Fire Dept. won't hear of it.

I sit waiting for my analyst in the reception room. I am hungrier than I remember being in my adult life, but it is only 9:30 in the morning. I bought a jug of yogurt, and I quietly sit and consume copious amounts of the plain white variety. He comes to call me into his office and casually asks if I am missing my mom today.

After the sobs abate, I accuse him of the lowest trick in *An Introductory Guide to Psychoanalysis;* sure, I say, ask anyone this as an opening question, and you instantly have a session. But why me? And why just today? The answer comes slowly.

"I opened the door," he says, "and witnessed you with a blank stare, shoveling the closest thing I know to mother's milk into your mouth."

Today is May 3rd. In ten days it will be a memory, and my blue dress will go up on blocks. All rites and passages will be successfully observed and celebrated. My son will move into manhood, and I will muddle through some of the clean up and *all* of the motherhood.

Threshold

✳ Curiously mowed field beyond barn threshold. Peninsula, Ohio.

My Son Wakes Me Up

My son wakes me up.

I don't mean just wakes me up, and I don't mean he's a little baby who needs to be fed.

My son wakes me up. On purpose. Loudly. Directly. And unceasingly. He is a very intelligent child, with cool reflections and cutting humor. He is able to remember things I cannot even recall being told. He uses the name of a person we only met in passing. He has a prodigious memory. And yet, we have gone over why he should not wake me up on every single morning, over and over again; he nods his little gnome-shaped six-year-old head; he blinks his ageless eyes and agrees. He agrees with me! He agrees that I have done a lot that day and I'll probably still be doing laundry or some sort of food service or reading much longer into the night. So we decide together that waking me up at the crack of dawn would not be fair. This, I say, is a tactic used in interrogation. Prisoners of war are constantly awakened until they just crack. There's that word again. I'm afraid of cracking. Always have been. There is a time right after a baby comes, at least there was for me with my firstborn, where I was certain that he knew exactly when he was losing me. There is a moment when I would begin to slip into the deep folds of alpha sleep. That is the precise moment when he would cry. They are connected to us. The cord that was recently severed in a room somewhere now seems to snake around hallways, elongating with the movement of his bed away from mine. So I bring him closer in the hopes of actually waking up, tending to him, and going "back to sleep" before I could actually remember my own name. No such luck with what I face now. He wakes me up. And he wakes me up in a fashion that suggests an emergency.

I try to determine the nature of the emergency he *feels* inside of him, because clearly there is not one in the real world. He cannot say. Sometimes he says he forgot. Ha. Sometimes he tells me *why* he needs me, but it falls flat. They are all reasons that we have worked out beforehand. He is perfectly capable of getting his own breakfast, playing alone, and he loves to read. I always leave his latest favorite book right by his bedside where he can easily find it. But he wakes me up. He is immediately remorseful, and I can almost hear how sorry he is through the ringing in my ears that is caused by the sudden rush of blood to my head sped up by the clenched fist that is pounding on my heart inside of my chest. I can almost hear the answers to the questions I manage to ask through my locked jaw as the sunlight cuts its way through the littlest gap in the curtains and slices the pillow I was sleeping on in half. Almost. But not quite. I want to ignore him. I want to ignore him, but I want to understand him even more.

Einstein and Economics

N. came to me this morning, sad, somewhat resigned. His passion for astronomy, which has been so apparent over the last year, is waning. This from the boy who awoke at 3 A.M., dressed in the darkness, and, telescope in tow, hiked to the top of the wooded hill behind our farm to see Saturn, Jupiter, and the Moon line up and take a bow—one hour before dawn. This from the boy who, on July 4th as all the other kids were getting completely wired up, running around waiting for fireworks to explode, could be seen off to the side, reading Albert Einstein's *Essays in Science* and occasionally gazing upward in anticipation.

UNDISCOVERED

What happened?

It seemed to him, on this night, that everything had already been discovered. He was remembering when a nephew of a friend who was supposed to be showing him the astronomy equipment at the M.I.T. labs informed him that it was a nowhere field. All figured out. He was in the process of switching to economics, he said. The rise and fall of the market interested him more. That was the future.

Not so long ago, after he had pulled his wagon up the path leading to the high meadow, we heard the wagon coming back down the gravel drive. He had been gone for about three hours. When he got in the house and took off his many layers of clothing, we asked him how it had gone, and he told us that he had forgotten the all-important lens for his large telescope.

"Well, what did you do up there all this time?" A. asked.

"I saw what I could see."

Tonight N. is struggling to remember what was so great, so interesting, so compelling to him, even up to a week ago.

I tried feebly to explore the possibility that these deflated feelings are important moments in the spectrum of growth and discovery; they provide an opportunity, a "space" for something new. Take a shooting star for example. How can so much romance be attributed to a dying thing? We cannot always control passion; we can only feed it while it exists; witnessing its descent can be as important as heralding its arrival. The trick is to stave off the panic and the need for quick answers and action. Those are reserved for the floor of the stock exchange.

How Long

How long have I been weeding this same garden?

Now, on the solstice, I traipse out to the faded red
  shed.

(Remember that dream of painting something red

before the first white cover fell?)

While I was watching varsity basketball games and
  renting tuxedos,

the earth reclaimed my closely tended perennials—

  that laugh in the face of their name—

Somewhere in that missed year, which ends up being
  two,

UNDISCOVERED

my garden tools have also escaped—
they are living in the past.
Lying in the corner of the webbed darkness,
I find a miniature set—a pint-sized shovel and an
elf's hoe.
They are not rusted, having hardly been used by the
child that grew like a weed.

Big Night

I thought when my father died, I would feel more life. As if with his passing, I would be nudged toward something more essential. I sit on a log, thinking now of how I felt when my ma died, and I do not have the same feeling.

I walked up through the woods as the sun was setting. Being December 25th, it was quite rapidly growing dark. Orange streaks lit the ridgeline to the west. I felt to turn back, but as I did, I noticed the field through the blackened trees looked almost wheat-colored with light. It was peculiar that the light could bounce this way—how deeply nestled in the woods this field is—so I walked on. As I came over the rise, I saw the source of the light: a full white moon shone down on that field.

How I ran from my home when I was so young—to follow the sun—and how hot it got. How brightly lit each turn was, and when I sensed it setting, I, too, settled into homes and ways of being, believing.

The moon is on the rise, and the path will once again be lit. The color is a bit different, bluer with the passage of time. A new way of seeing is required, a relaxed eye, able to navigate the darkness as well as the light.

My father's death is not just to be chalked up as another loss. It is not my loss. I was his. Each child reminds us that we will move on, and each child, too, will sit on a log one day watching the moon rise over the upper field.

Later that night I took B. on an owling expedition. When we reached the upper field, the frost had settled, and it glistened in the moonlight like so many diamonds. Big night for the field.

Summer in a Lifeboat

I t is the middle of a late August night, and we are sleeping with all the windows open. The sound comes first, and we flip on the outside light. The apple tree is shaking, and as we watch it, the bird feeder, a long tubular one that A. had tricked out in such a way as to be impervious to attacks from squirrels and other ground-sharing rodents, is disappearing slowly up into the tree. It seems as if its suspending wire is pulling it up. This is followed by a loud thump.

By the time we get downstairs to the kitchen and throw on the brightest light, the 250-pound black bear is staring right at me through the kitchen window. I am staring into its bewildered face just before it runs back into the woods that line our home.

I am laughing as hard as I have laughed for a while. I look over at A. He has been outside, yelling at the bear. I laugh even harder at this. The times I have felt like a *team* with my husband are often out of a cartoon. We are hanging off of some cliff somewhere, hoping the little branch we are grasping onto will hold.

Now I feel a rush of tears about to come. This can happen with a good laugh. I try not to worry too awful much where it is coming from—if it is a deep laugh, things that scare me and other things that I must have misplaced earlier are vying for position. It feels a little like laughing in the face of death.

I sob openly on the heels of a good laugh like this. It can be a safe time to slip it by without frightening people too much. In this case, my husband would not blink. He has visited that address himself.

There is the lore of the Inuit when hunting a bear: He takes a wolf bone and whittles a point at each end and places it in a piece of blubber. It is left for the bear on his hunting trail. He will find it there and eat it. Within days, the bear will grow weak and as he travels, he will leave a bloody trail from the bone's damage—it is cutting and killing him slowly from the inside.

The summer of 2002 arrived in a lifeboat, buckets of rain fell, and sometimes it felt as if I would never stop crying. Some were tears of joy and triumph for having made it through, and although threadbare, whole. Some were tears of shame for what I had not respected about life.

We had been making a film in Mississippi. A. was directing, and I had a small role but was there with all our boys for their summer break from school.

One day, the producer waited in the bushes outside of our rented home in Oxford until A. had left for work. He knocked on the door. My son came to get me in the shower and said that the "producer guy is at the front door, and he is crying."

This is *never* good.

What transpired next can only be told in Rashomon-type vignettes—but to me, the important part was this:

If you walk in any direction for fifteen minutes in the south, you are bound to come upon a cemetery. So when my husband and I set out that night after dinner, to walk and talk about the fact that the production had announced it was "out of money" and in fact had nothing to pay the crew for even one day, a decision needed to be reached. We came across a large cemetery that dated back to the Civil War. Sometimes, for perspective on a problem, take a walk in a cemetery.

We stayed and finished that film. I ended up line producing, a job I can understand only in wartime, or as a sort of punishment. But we did it, of our own volition and with some panache. I still contend that you do not really know how to make something until you take it apart.

We premiered that film at the Toronto Film Festival on 9/10/01.

It is hard to look at bitterness with a different outcome than that Inuit bear will have. It is essential to do the laugh check— How much does it hurt when you laugh these days? I am watching the bear galumph up the hill on three legs, with our bird feeder under his big, fat, fourth paw. My husband is naked on the front porch, peering into the night, and I figure the bone is not stuck just yet. Disappointment is a misplaced hope. But bitterness will kill you.

Aging Gracefully

The term "aging gracefully" has always given me pause. It sounds as if one is lingering on each landing of a descending staircase, waving elegantly. The descent is what I do not like. Aging, I feel, is more of an ascension. It denotes a process that is alive and happening, growing up and getting closer, moving toward the essential: What was there in the beginning and will be there in the end. We spend a lot of time in between trying to mask the physical aspects, hide it, reshape it, but it usually looks just that way . . . an altered state.

I have tried in the last decade to abstain from value judgments on those who choose surgical processes. I don't know enough about them to even remark. Sometimes they are star-tling to the untrained eye, but many times I'm sure I don't know what has been done.

I am interested in the process of aging as an unfolding of some mystery. When I was little, someone told me that when you age, you turn into the person you were all your life. My grandmother, although possessing beautiful skin, had a sort of permanent grimace that she called her smile. It did things to her face that said a lot. I didn't get to see my mother age past sev-enty, though she had a twinkle in her eye that stole your atten-tion immediately.

Each time I travel to another country and encounter another culture, when I return I am struck by how much American cul-ture is led by the media and not the lives and inherent beauty of its general population. Popular culture has no room for real wrinkles. The movie industry in the United States promotes a lineless, motionless look for women of all ages that is so com-pletely nonthreatening as to be, ironically, scary. We are the spe-cialists in no lines, no map, no history, including the history of many other lands.

My favorite state of mind is when I am not made to think about myself from the outside. Through the events early in my life, the message that I got about vision is that you will never truly know what you look like to others, because it is your consciousness and your critical eye that is looking in the mirror. It is simply a measure of one's own compassion for oneself, which we all know is the first step to compassion for others.

It seems to me that the challenge is to be the embodiment of whatever is happening in your life at the moment. Sad faces can be extraordinarily moving and beautiful. Happiness is a message not a look.

Can beauty, enhanced or not, be palpable without acceptance of oneself at every stage of life? I am interested in this question. The effects of our actions are written on our faces. Why not tell countless stories in many languages?

Ganesh

Recently, I traveled to India with Sightsavers International, an aid organization I have been working with. This was my first trip to India. Within an hour of my arrival in New Delhi, I knew that I was in a situation that required my immediate attention. It involved road safety. The craziness of Italy; the broken and treacherous roads of Kenya; the nonexistent roads of Niger; the narrow, winding paths of China and Tibet; the primitive quality of Indonesia; and the overly empowered personality of New York drivers could not have prepared me for the hair-raising nightmare that I would come to know as "travel" in India. My willingness, because of the kind of work we do in challenging locations, was now putting the fact of my mortality front row center. I felt that the work I had volunteered for had expanded from an acceptance of a lack of creature comforts to my very life. And it was in the hands of virtual strangers. I knew I would never be behind the wheel of any of these vehicles nor at ease in any other seat in the car. There were no obvious laws of the road: no signs, no lanes, and no consistency of vehicles. On any given day, one shares the narrow roads with high-speed buses hell-bent to keep some unknown schedule, horse-drawn carts, pedicabs, Indy 500–style drivers behind the wheels of wildly overstuffed cars, hay being transported on camel carts, and the occasional stray cow, which is always allotted the right-of-way.

I came to notice, over the first three days, due to my inability to look out past the windshield, that each car I entered (mantra in my heart, prayer on my lips) had a consistency to the dashboard's arrangement. They all held some form, whether it was an actual statuette or a colorful drawing, of the Hindu elephant god, Ganesh.

As a seasoned traveler who is used to giving myself over to local customs, I made a quick executive decision to join in and give my trust over to the divine powers of Ganesh. I would look to Ganesh to deliver me home safely to my family. I placed a trinket or a flower, discreetly plucked at the last moment, below his watchful eyes and elegant trunk. As the days went on, this really seemed to be working. Miraculously, I would lie down each night to go to sleep, safe in the knowledge that I had made a wise decision.

So the fact that I found myself, in the third week, on the River Ganges, in the delta region known as the Sunderbans, where the river meets the Bay of Bengal, on a boat, at sunset, with no Ganesh in sight, left me a little more than worried.

The sunset was beautiful, poetic even, as it was a full moon and the winter solstice. But as I soon learned through our inter-preter, this was not a river to be on after darkness fell, with a boat-man who was unfamiliar with the small motorboat that had been donated to ferry patients more easily from island to island (there are fifty-four such islands) for treatment. There were no lights, and it was impossible to calculate the depth of the water, which as a rule is quite shallow in this crocodile-infested area. My first idea (there were to be many racing through my mind) was to suggest that we give up trying to find our original destination, as late as we now were, and just pull over to land before we ran out of gas (there was no more after the spare two-gallon can at my feet) and camp for the night. This idea, when I found voice enough to utter it as a plan, was quickly laughed off, as no one knew the exact boundaries of the large tiger preserve that makes this area of India one of the most mystical. It is home to the honey catchers, many of whom now roam the forests with large chunks of their bodies missing from successfully "catching" the honey, while not so successfully eluding the pursuing tiger.

Although I had some degree of amusement at the fact that I was living a Zen parable, the choice between a crocodile and a tiger brought me to thinking about my family. I found myself, as difficult as it was, working my way through each one and imagining them going on without me. I saw them in their grief, struggling to make sense of how I'd left. I was compelled to make it all come out okay for them in my own mind. My oldest in college, knowing that I had helped him learn to trust his heart and to use his rich mind, finding power in his passions and humor in the everyday life of those he'd work with and help along the way; my stepson who had weathered the storm of an incoming parent he did not expect (what kid does?) and how my loyalty would read as meddling and sometimes irk him, wishing instead I would just leave him be. My youngest, just eight, now facing the broken heart of losing a parent too young but remembering the travels we shared together and my voice, which doesn't always sound friendly, coming to him in confusing moments as a help and a source of unconditional love. I visualized my husband, as close as I was able to imagine my life without him, a certain emptiness but then filled with a responsibility to our love that would now include seeing the kids through and honoring our own lives and pursuit of passion and understanding. I saw him making things without me and going on. All this, and when I was finished, we were still chugging through dark waters, mist now settling in like some mythic fog creating a no-man's land.

What happened next, I have come to know in my life in different ways—through nature and poetry, through art or music, falling in love, an accident or the death of a friend—things that have broken through the routine of daily life to bear a call that I could hear, a call that seemed to resonate with some question in my soul. In retrospect, I have come to call some of these moments close calls. I, too, have used it as the common idiom it is known for. I had never investigated it further. It is widely known as a sports term—too close to call. Alternately it is a divine, spiritual, or sacred appointment or a prompting to a special service. But why do we seem to hear the call most closely when we are in peril? On the Ganges, I pursued the call as a mother would. I felt the need to quickly complete what I might not get to do in real time. And although I felt like I had succeeded for myself, I realized I had held back some of my finer observations with my kids in deference to their ages and their developing judgment, which needed its own natural speed to grow. And upon that very reflection, thinking about how much I would like to tell one of my sons about a song I had heard that reminded me of his facility with language and how he should apply that to his music, I was transported back to my own seventeen, and how at that precarious age, I lay in a hospital bed, partially paralyzed and unable to see, hearing another call that felt like peace and freedom from the pain that would most certainly greet me should I decide to wake up. And through the denial of that call, and the intention to suffer through whatever was coming, I answered my mother, who beckoned me from the side of my bed.

So what of these two calls? How close is a close call if we do not let it change our lives? I do believe that they are there to do just that: change us in a way that allows us to connect the things that have wanted to come back together because they belong together. I now know that one must live in a state of readiness, of listening, however differently we define the terms of it, so that when there is a call, close or distant, we can choose to answer. (The fact that I would not have been on the Ganges working for an organization called Sightsavers in the first place had I not been in that accident thirty years before is all I need to know about how things work.)

The call heard so closely as a young girl, and always kept in my heart did not stop me from pursuing a dream or two in the world. One does not sacrifice to respond. It makes one *more* capable, *more* willing, and less fearful.

On my last day in India, as we were careening through the streets to make a 4 A.M. flight from Calcutta to London, I smiled at the driver and said, "Well I might have gotten upset had I not seen a Ganesh on your dashboard, but I know now that I'll be okay." He laughed and informed me, "Oh, Ganesh does not protect you that way. Ganesh is the remover of obstacles."

Boathouse with Portal

✳ Unseaworthy and overturned. A boat becomes a house in Lindesfarne. Northumberland, United Kingdom.

Outside

It occurs to me,

while clearing the broken in the last

ice storm branches from the faded

carpet of grass, geese honking at the

winter white sun,

that I don't write

because I'm not outside.

There Are No Poems

There are no poems now
no slamming screen doors
while the Santa Anas blow through
the moon full and high
does not throw daytime shadows
on my son's room.
I climb the stairs and
my mother says hello
from the predawn silent sky.

I have no pain in my chest
no unnecessary little accidents.
The coyotes do not howl in the distant hills.
I answer to my name as it
comes in on the wind.

Grand Entrance

☀ Sentry tents, Ottoman style. Erected by the king in 1781. Haga Park, Stockholm, Sweden.

High-Strung Religion

I have been obsessed for over twenty years with an image—
both as metaphor and as fact. And now I was to meet the
man who has been emblematic, watch him walk on a wire
across a gorge of the Grand Canyon, and write about it. Not to
mention the adventure of five days, driving through the scenery
to find him, King of the Clandestine. Away from hearth and
home, I would reflect on all aspects of my preoccupation with
the "Ascensioniste."

It was in honor of this occasion that I purchased a yellow
unicycle. I had strong memories of riding one as a child—how I
had to lean forward, finding a center that seemed anywhere but

in the middle. I remembered how to mount it by placing the pedals parallel and applying equal pressure to both. I rode with surprising ease for about fifteen minutes, and then had a terrible vision: It was my brother. *He* was the one who rode the unicycle, not me. I promptly fell.

The word *pilgrimage* comes to mind. A long journey made by a pilgrim to a holy place or shrine.

Or wire.

I was now dreaming of it. I would awake at dawn, sun rays cutting a sharp line over the top of the Catskill Mountains, with a searing pain in my foot. It began between my big toe and second toe and extended back through my foot and out the heel. It ached; too much identification with the subject. He's walking. You're writing.

As I went about my maternal duties, singing of Those Daring Young Men and juggling schedules, I would wonder where he was. Was he hanging from a harness somewhere, securing bowlines, with meat hooks dangling about his neck—testing the core or "soul" of the wire that would be his perfect catenary path?

(My own past has had so many turns. Trying as I have, always to nod to the left and the right while praying to remain awake in the middle—keeping passion and concentration alive to pull me forward.)

Now I am childlike in my excitement. Oh, Philippe Petit! You are walking again—yet you defy pedestrianism. After an unapproved walk between the Trade Towers in New York City, you were arrested at your destination. When asked by the judge why you did what you did, you replied, "When I see three oranges, I must juggle; when I see two towers, I must walk."

All the years I had worked on films and had felt the perfect metaphor for what I was doing in what you were doing—the grace and uselessness of it all—perchance, the art.

Oh, equilibrist—relaxed in a storm—lying still, up high.

At my most unstable, remembering Karl Wallenda standing on his head atop a wire, high over Georgia, and saying later that he did it for Vietnam.

What a strange and compelling breed, the aerealist.

High above the questions swirling around abandoned solutions.

High above the homeless children with untreated earaches—showing up at a school unable to hear.

High above for good reason.

One cannot write about it as "levity." It is grounded in High-Strung Religion for the Balance Challenged, with guy wires of faith and freedom. You have said (not to me, of course, we had never met), "Every thought on the wire leads to a fall."

I cannot think of this anymore. They called me today to say you had postponed your walk for a year. I hung up the phone dizzy with descent.

I considered peppering your answering machine with accusations and taunts. I felt the hot tears of a childhood disappointment.

(Coaxed out of a hiding place with the promise of a new kite to fly, I was whisked away to the doctor's office for a shot instead.)

Where is my kite?

Where is my unicycle?

I take it out to the driveway and stay up longer than ever this time—I don't have a thought in my head.

You are still with me when I land.

I walk out to my garden and tie up the weighty tomatoes, cinching them with a tripod lashing.

If I made my pilgrimage, I console myself, my garden would have gone to seed anyway. It's good I won't be wandering around sacred Native American tribal grounds somewhere in Arizona in a rented car with an outdated map that my twelve-year-old son had found in a pile of discarded *National Geographics* on a New York City curb one summer night.

Besides, my photographer tore a ligament in her knee last week. It's fine. What's my little pilgrimage anyway, you were walking on a wire sixteen hundred feet above the ground.

I pull in the clean clothes off the low line and walk to the barn to begin my chores. I'm sure you had a good reason for canceling.

Weather conditions.

Land (air?) disputes with Native Americans.

Existential Anxiety.

UNDISCOVERED

A broken toe.

It occurs to me that you may walk anyway. This is some sort of ploy; you are not wont to do this for the crowd, but for God, for the Devil, and for the Wild Blue Yonder. I await word from any of the three.